MOMENTS WITH ONESELF SEF

VEDANTA 24x7

SWAMI DAYANANDA SARASWATI
Arsha Vidya

Arsha Vidya
Research and Publication Trust
Chennai

Published by :
Arsha Vidya Research
and Publication Trust
4 'Sri Nidhi' Apts 3rd Floor
Sir Desika Road Mylapore
Chennai 600 004 INDIA
Tel : 044 2499 7023
Telefax : 2499 7131
Email : avrandpc@gmail.com
Website: avrpt.com

ISBN : 978-81-904203-6-5

First Edition :	August	2007	Copies : 2000
1st Reprint :	February	2008	Copies : 5000
2nd Reprint :	June	2011	Copies : 1000

Design & format:
Graaphic Design

Printed at :
Sudarsan Graphics
27, Neelakanta Mehta Street
T. Nagar, Chennai 600 017
Email : info@sudarsan.com

Contents

Key to Transliteration and Pronunciation of Sanskrit Letters

Sanskrit is a highly phonetic language and hence accuracy in articulation of the letters is important. For those unfamiliar with the *Devanāgari* script, the international transliteration is a guide to the proper pronunciation of Sanskrit letters.

अ	*a*	*(but)*
आ	*ā*	*(father)*
इ	*i*	*(it)*
ई	*ī*	*(beat)*
उ	*u*	*(full)*
ऊ	*ū*	*(pool)*
ऋ	*ṛ*	*(rhythm)*
ॠ	*ṝ*	*(marine)*
ऌ	*ḷ*	*(revelry)*
ए	*e*	*(play)*
ऐ	*ai*	*(aisle)*
ओ	*o*	*(go)*
औ	*au*	*(laud)*
क	*ka*	*(seek)* 1
ख	*kha*	*(blockhead)**1
ग	*ga*	*(get)* 1
घ	*gha*	*(log hut)**1
ङ	*ṅa*	*(sing)* 1
च	*ca*	*(chunk)* 2
छ	*cha*	*(catch him)**2
ज	*ja*	*(jump)* 2
झ	*jha*	*(hedgehog)**2
ञ	*ña*	*(bunch)* 2
ट	*ṭa*	*(true)**3
ठ	*ṭha*	*(anthill)**3
ड	*ḍa*	*(drum)**3
ढ	*ḍha*	*(godhead)**3
ण	*ṇa*	*(under)**3
त	*ta*	*(path)**4
थ	*tha*	*(thunder)**4
द	*da*	*(that)**4
ध	*dha*	*(breathe)**4
न	*na*	*(nut)**4
प	*pa*	*(put)* 5
फ	*pha*	*(loophole)**5
ब	*ba*	*(bin)* 5
भ	*bha*	*(abhor)**5
म	*ma*	*(much)* 5
य	*ya*	*(loyal)*
र	*ra*	*(red)*
ल	*la*	*(luck)*
व	*va*	*(vase)*
श	*śa*	*(sure)*
ष	*ṣa*	*(shun)*
स	*sa*	*(so)*
ह	*ha*	*(hum)*

ं	ṁ	*anusvāra*	(nasalisation of preceding vowel)
:	ḥ	*visarga*	(aspiration of preceding vowel)
*			No exact English equivalents for these letters

1.	Guttural	–	Pronounced from throat
2.	Palatal	–	Pronounced from palate
3.	Lingual	–	Pronounced from cerebrum
4.	Dental	–	Pronounced from teeth
5.	Labial	–	Pronounced from lips

The 5th letter of each of the above class – called nasals – are also pronounced nasally.

Accommodating others

Vedanta is the teaching of the reality of oneself. It is in the form of inquiry wherein one discovers the real meaning of the word 'I' the self that remains unchanged from childhood to youth to old age. It leads one to discover that the unchanged self is free from any form of limitation. To recognise and own this wholeness one requires a prepared mind. For the one with an unprepared mind, Vedanta is like calculus for a person who is still learning basic mathematics. In Vedanta the prepared mind is one that has in relative measure, what it seeks to discover in the absolute sense. If the self is absolute contentment, then the mind of the seeker must be relatively content. If the self is absolute love, then the seeker must be relatively a loving person, a person who happily accepts people and things as they are.

To gain such a mind implies the recognition, the importance and the understanding of certain values and attitudes. For instance, accommodating others is one such value. In fact, anger is due to lack of accommodation. If you expect the world to conform to your liking, then it is your own expectation that brings anger to you. Accommodation is an understanding that the other person behaves as he or she does because the person cannot act contrary to his or her background. You have no right to expect something different from someone just because it suits your needs. If you think you have a right to ask someone to change, then that person equally has the right to ask you to let him or her live as he or she does. In fact, only by accommodating others, allowing them to be what they are, do you gain a relative freedom in your day-to-day life.

In many ways, everyone interferes in everyone else's life. Everyone creates a global effect by his or her actions. Ordinarily, you just look at things from a small perspective, and you find the person you are angry with, looming large before you. In fact, you are never free from anyone's influence or from all the forces in the universe; nor can you perform an action without affecting everyone else. Even our statements will affect others. Therefore, our freedom needs to include the fact that we are all inter-related.

Even the Swami is not free. A couple passed by when I was at a zoo, and the man remarked to his partner, "Look at this one." I was the one with these strange clothes to be looked at. People often make such comments. I try not to disturb people, but it seems that my clothes, the traditional robes of a renunciate, cause a slight disturbance. I have made a decision, and it will definitely affect others. If I am disturbed by others' comment, then I gain only that much freedom that they grant me. However, if I reverse the process, if I give the freedom to others to be what they are, to that extent I am free. So, I do not argue with them. My freedom is the freedom that I give to them to have their opinion about me, which is different from the fact. Thus, there are benefits in accommodating people as they are.

If someone makes a comment about you, allow him or her to do so. If the comment is not true, you usually try to justify your actions and prove him or her wrong. If you are objective, you will try to see if there is any validity in the person's criticism of you. If someone has put you down for his or her own security, give the person that freedom; you are then free. What tightening can you do to a bolt when the threads are not there? The world can disturb you only to the extent you allow the world to disturb you. You do not allow the world to disturb you if you give the world the freedom to do what it wants within the rules of society. By changing yourself totally in this way you gain, according to your value for accommodation, relatively abiding contentment and freedom.

Practising accommodation you come to terms with yourself psychologically, with yourself as a personality. That is what we call *yoga-sādhana*. Look back at the situations, the people and events that disturbed you in your life. They are not mere memories but remnants of reactions. A reaction is not something you do consciously. You cannot consciously get angry, for anger is not an action but a reaction that takes place, something you have no control over. Reactions create a great impact on you and become part of your psyche. They are aspects of the personality of a person. In fact, they are false, born of a lack of alertness on your part. Memory itself is not unpleasant. Unpleasantness is there in your mind because of lingering reactions and emotions, which have become as though real. Therefore, recall those people and moments that caused you pain. Perhaps, you carry guilt because of some hurt you caused another. In the seat of meditation recall them all and let them be as they are. With patience you free yourself from all residuals of the reactions.

When you look at the blue sky and the stars, or the birds and mountains, you have no complaints about them and you are happy. You see the rocks on the riverbed; they did not do anything to please you.

Yet you are happy because you accept them as they are, and therefore you are pleased. The river flows in its own way; it does not bother you, if you do not expect its fullness to be greater or to flow in a different direction. In fact, you seek out natural spots because they do not invoke the displeased person, the angry, and the hard-to-please person that you seem to be. They do not strike the demanding cord in you. You are one with the situation, an accommodating self, without the need of the world doing anything to please you.

Thus, you are a pleased person with reference to a few things. It is the wedge you have to create in yourself. When you go to the mountains, the mountains do nothing to please you but you find you are pleasing to yourself. See how pleased you can be, and bring that pleased person to bear upon all situations and the people who had displeased you and whom you had displeased at one time or another. Then look at yourself just as you would when you look at nature. Accept others as you accept the stars. Pray for a change if you think you or they need to change, and do what you can to promote change. But accept others first. Only in this way can you really change. Accept others totally and you are free; then you discover love, which is yourself.

The human being alone, among the sentient beings, is self-conscious and unprogrammed. You are aware of yourself, your environment and you are free to change your attitude and behaviour. Self-awareness and free will are unique to a human being. All other beings on this planet are tied to a pattern set by their instincts. A human, too, has instincts but he or she is not bound by their pattern. In fact, blessed with a free will, you cannot merely rely upon instinct as a guide for your behaviour, but must thoughtfully choose the actions in accordance with the ethical standards. If you allow your actions to happen, triggered by instinct-born impulses or some conditioned mechanical-ness, you are not acting but merely reacting.

All reactions are happenings. Human choice is over action, not reaction. Once I act I have no power to choose the reaction. I can choose to clap my hands or not. However, when the palms of my hands contact each other with a certain velocity, I have no option to decide when they make a noise. A reaction is like that. Any reaction is determined by the totality of laws and circumstances that, once an action has occurred, come into force to make the given reaction happen.

If I fail to choose my actions consciously and deliberately, but simply let them happen, there will be reactions, either impulsive reactions born of instincts or mechanical reactions born of conditioning. In either case, it is that special faculty that makes me human, namely choice of action based on rational thought.

So what? Why does it matter whether I exercise this special faculty? Is there a reason why I should consciously choose my actions? What is wrong with letting impulse or conditioning guide me? My impulses are normal. My conditioning, carried by my parents, my teachers, and society, is good. That may be true. Yet, over any period of time, a life based on impulsive or mechanical behaviour will run into problems. When my actions are really reactions, my mind will be troubled, because experience will not teach me. Conflicts between thought and deed will bother me. Painful emotions will build up. Mood will be my master. When I consciously, rationally choose my actions, I am in a position to benefit from what has happened before. Experience is my teacher. Even from wrong actions I become wiser. However, when I let my actions happen, I am not consciously there to learn from the past.

In addition, these actions that are happenings will lead to a split in me. No matter how constructive my conditioning may have been my impulses will not always be in line with my ethical standards, leading to behaviour in conflict with values. Action in conflict will produce a mind divided against it. Like Duryodhana in the *Mahābhārata*, I will find myself saying, "*jānāmi dharmaṁ na ca me pravṛttiḥ jānāmi adharmaṁ na ca me nivṛttiḥ*, I know what is right, but I cannot do it. I know what is not right, I cannot but do it."

Duryodhana had lost the power of rational choice over his actions. His mind was in conflict and split between values and impulses. A mind in conflict is always a painful mind.

Pain, in fact, is the companion of many reactions. When I analyse the attitudes and conduct that all religions condemn as bad, I find that bad actions are really painful actions. Universally condemned emotions, such as jealousy and hatred, are built up from reactions. These are disturbing emotions that trouble the mind. No one consciously chooses to be jealous or hateful. Such actions grow from the license granted to impulse. Impulse stems from desire, longing for the agreeable, and anger, aversion to the disagreeable.

In the *Gītā*, Lord Kṛṣṇa says:[1] "The one who is able to master the force born of anger and desire here in the world, before release from the body, is a *karma-yogin*. He indeed is a happy person."

Finally, to the extent my actions are the result of impulse, I will be ruled by moods. With mood as my master I will be a question mark to others and myself. No one can know whether at any given time I will be reasonable, touchy, co-operative or stubborn.

Thus, analysis shows that thoughtless action, born of impulse or conditioning, will cause me pain and problems. If I see this but find that I am caught in a web of reactions and mechanical-ness, what can I do? I can undertake a program of alertness.

I can commit myself to watch consciously, all my thoughts, my words, and my actions, no matter how small, trivial or insignificant they are. To be conscious of all thoughts, words, and actions is called *tapas* in Sanskrit. The word is used to cover many religious austerities such as fasting, observing silence, and similar disciplines. The purpose of all these disciplines

---

[1] *śaknotīhaiva yaḥ soḍhuṁ prāk śarīravimokṣaṇāt*
kāmakrodhodbhavaṁ vegaṁ sa yuktaḥ sa sukhī naraḥ (5: 23)

is only to make one more conscious. When one is doing something different from one's routine, one's alertness and awareness get sharpened.

With sharpened awareness I will be able to recognise when I am mechanical. If I become conscious that I am mechanical, then mechanical-ness ceases. With mechanical-ness gone, my actions are subject to my choice. I can choose deliberately to align even my trivial thoughts, words, and deeds so that they are not at war with one another. Mastery over small things brings, in its wake, control over large ones. Through alertness and deliberateness, I can free myself from reactions born of impulse and conditioning.

A mind free from reactions is quiet, receptive, objective, capable, and serene. Such a mind enjoys relative happiness. It can learn from experience, not fraught with conflict. One can deal with negative emotions and one is no more subject to moods. One with that kind of a mind is ready to discover the truth of the self through the teaching of Vedanta.

I perform an action out of a desire to accomplish something, but when the action does not produce the result, I am found to have difficulty in accepting it. Having a desire or acting on it is not the problem. My attitude towards the result of my action may cause a problem. If it is more than what I expected, I am elated; if it is equal to my expectation, I am satisfied; if it is less than I expected, I am dissatisfied; and if it is opposite of what I expected, I am depressed.

I may be able to deal with a contrary result once. Yet, if it happens a few times, I consider myself a failure. Therefore, people falsely accuse desire as the problem. In reality, my attitude towards the result of an action is the problem. If I accept the result with the proper attitude, then a desire does not cause any problem.

In the *Gītā*, Lord Kṛṣṇa says:[2] "Your choice is in action only, never in the results. Do not take yourself to be the author of the results of action. Let your attachment not be to inaction."

---

[2] *karmaṇyevādhikāraste mā phaleṣu kadācana*
mā karmaphalaheturbhūrmā te saṅgo'stvakarmaṇi (2: 47)

The laws of physics and bio-energy control the movement of my hand. The laws of psychology control my emotional state. Similarly, my actions produce results, according to certain laws. I perform actions and I am responsible for them, but the results are given to me. It is the laws that always govern the results of my action.

It is often mistakenly thought that one should not expect a result while performing actions. Every human being performs action expecting results. When I take a step forward, I expect the result of moving forward. When I eat, I expect the food to be digested. In fact, I act purely for the sake of the result. Otherwise, I need not act at all. It is said, "*prayojanam anuddiśya mando'pi na pravartate*, even a dull-witted person does not engage in action without expecting a result."

The Lord Gives the Results

I find this world that I live in is well designed. All beings in this world are equipped for survival. Fishes have gills to breathe and the human beings have nostrils to inhale air.

Every object in this world has its place in the scheme of things, being intelligently put together and each object is further reducible into its constituents.

The shirt that one wears is made of cloth, the cloth of fibres; every fibre of molecules; every molecule of atoms, and so on. Thus, the world, being put together, is a creation. Is there a cause for this intelligent, meaningful creation? Is there a creator?

For any creation, there must be a creator who knows exactly what he or she is going to create and the purpose of the creation. A potter knows what a pot is and how to make it. He has all the knowledge and skill for this. Similarly, there must be a creator who has the knowledge of the entire creation and the power to create it. There is an efficient cause, *nimitta kāraṇa*, for this creation.

To create anything, I not only require the knowledge and the skill to make it, but I also require the material with which to create. Without clay, the potter cannot make clay pots. Similarly, the creator of this world requires the material to create with. This material cannot be distinct from the efficient cause, the creator. If it were, someone must have created that material. This someone then must be the new creator. Where did this creator find the material to create? Thus, we face the logical absurdity of infinite regress if we continue with this line of reasoning. Therefore, the efficient cause must also be the material out of which this world is created. The material cause, *upādāna kāraṇa,* and the efficient cause both together, rests in the Lord, Īśvara. The Lord is the efficient and material cause of this creation. This is the Vedic vision of the Lord.

Every creation is non-separate from its material. From this we can clearly understand that the world is non-separate from the Lord. Everything in this world is the Lord, the laws of this world, the sense objects, my body, mind and senses. Thus, the Lord is the ultimate Giver of the results for our actions through the laws and that includes the law of *karma* too.

Prasāda buddhi
An attitude of glad acceptance

Anything that comes from the Lord can be looked upon as *prasāda. Prasāda* is not an object; it is an attitude towards an object. For instance, if you are a diabetic you are not supposed to eat sweets. A friend offers you a sweet, a *laddu,* and you refuse to take it. Then, he says it is from Lord Tirupati Bālāji. At once, your attitude towards the *laddu* changes completely. The recognition of the fact that the *laddu* is from an altar changes your attitude. You become a devotee humbly accepting what comes to you from the Lord.

You are ready to take things as they come. You are aware that the result may not conform to your expectations although you have done your best. Recognising that it is the Lord who gives everything, you are not overwhelmed by any situation. You are well prepared to face all situations with poise.

The vision of the Vedas, being what it is, advocates a lifestyle that is entirely unique. Since you are already a complete person, the tradition is only an aid to help you discover this profound truth. It is a great vision that everybody, wants and struggles for, in life. Nobody rests content with what he or she is. In spite of one's accomplishments and skills, one always has a sense of inadequacy. The adequacy one seeks is oneself alone. To discover this, however, one must be mature. Though physically one may be an adult, emotionally one can still remain a child. Adulthood does not assure emotional maturity. One can remain as angry, self-centred, jealous and hateful as one was in childhood. However, as an adult one has to grow out of these tendencies and become emotionally mature.

The Veda gives us a plan to make ourselves mature. It teaches a lifestyle and value structure that helps us grow so well that we can discover we are the 'whole'. Since it is based on knowledge, it is not confined to a culture of a particular time, nation, or geography. Knowledge is always true to the object and no one has a geographical claim over it.

Gaining knowledge is neither difficult nor easy. It appears difficult if you are not ready, but if you are, there is nothing easier. To know a given thing, you have to have a certain preparedness determined by what you want to know. In the case of the Vedas what you want to know is what you want to be. This is unlike any other knowledge. Naturally, you require a unique preparedness that the Vedas prescribe as a life of duties.

Duty-based Vedic society

Everybody has duties to perform in society. Tasks in the Vedic society were broadly brought under four heads. Any society must have someone to teach, to officiate the rituals. His dedication should be only to the pursuit of knowledge and his job to provide that knowledge to society. Even today, in any society, there is a class of people who are teachers, scientists, and who work to gather more knowledge. They are called *brāhmaṇa*s. The second type of job is that of administration, law, order and defence. This is to protect *dharma* since people abuse freedom. Those who implement this are the *kṣatriya*s. The third type of job deals with commerce, agriculture and cattle protection. This is very important in every society. Whether the system is based on barter or monetary system, there should be somebody who makes things available to buy or barter for. This community is that of the *vaiśya*s. The fourth job is to make all these possible and is done by the *śūdra*s. You will find these four corresponding types of people in every society.

Everyone has to work towards his or her self-discovery by neutralising his or her likes and dislikes. For this, he or she must give precedence to values, *dharma*. When your birth and family already determine your job, you need not compete in the society for another job; you just do what is to be done by you. Your father had this job and so did your grandfather; you do the same. However, if money is the criterion, the emphasis is different. You have to determine which job market is open and plan even your education accordingly. Thus, even education is profession-oriented and one's outlook, competitive.

The Veda outlines a life of duties. It cannot give a life of aggrandizement, hoarding, or success in terms of money and power. Even a king only performed his duties. Everyone's duties are called *sva-dharma*. If one chose another profession because of better monetary rewards, it was thought as a deviation from *sva-dharma*. In other words, there is no growth because the priority becomes money. Any system is subject to abuse and so is the *varṇa* system. Yet, while the system can become obsolete, the spirit of the system cannot. Even though we do not follow the system anywhere by birth, the four-fold spheres of work are always there. We have to understand only the spirit of the system. The spirit is duty.

The concept of duty cannot change, even though we have changed the forms. One's duty is determined by the situation one is in. Every situation warrants an action on one's part. If one is able to follow this, one is living one's *dharma*. In duty, there is nothing superior or inferior.

Every human being, in terms of disposition, is nothing but a combination of three qualities called *sattva, rajas,* and *tamas. Sattva* refers to thinking, conformity to values. When you are thinking or absorbed in devotional music, *sattva* is predominant. Everybody, including a habitual offender, has this quality, since he has love. *Rajas* is ambition, energy, desire, and hyper activity. *Tamas* is dullness. Everybody is a combination of these three. In this, any one quality can be predominant over the other two, giving rise to four dispositions. The first type has *sattva, rajas* and *tamas,* that is, *sattva* occupying the first place with *rajas* and *tamas,* taking the second and third place respectively. The second type has *rajas, sattva* and *tamas*. The third type has *rajas, tamas* and *sattva,* while the fourth has *tamas, rajas* and *sattva*.

The vision of the Veda is designed to make everyone's disposition predominantly *sattva,* the first category. Everybody has to become a *brāhmaṇa* by disposition, *guṇa*. A person who does the job of a *brāhmaṇa,* of performing *pūjā* in the temple with devotion is a *brāhmaṇa* by nature and also by action, *karma*. If he does the same thing for money and power, he is doing the job of a *brāhmaṇa,* but is a *vaiśya-brāhmaṇa*. If he does not even know how to do his job, he is a *śūdra-brāhmaṇa.* Similarly, there may be somebody sweeping the floor with great devotion. What he does is *śūdra-karma,* but that person is a *brāhmaṇa* by disposition. Performing *pūjā* is not superior to sweeping the floor. This is our culture. Any work, if understood as a duty, is complete, for it provides the individual the opportunity to become mature, to grow emotionally. If there is someone who is by disposition a *brāhmaṇa,* he has definitely made it as a mature person. We have to grow to be a *brāhmaṇa.* One action is no less efficacious than another in making a person mature, as long as it is performed with a sense of duty.

Duty and right

In the *Bhagavad Gītā* we see that one has to perform one's duties with the attitude of *yoga*. Traditionally, these duties go by one's *varṇa* and *āśrama*.

Even though the *varṇa* system is not viable today, we need to understand it. The Vedic spirit embodied in it is, "This is my duty toward the society, my family, my neighbours, the State, humanity, all the living beings, and even the *devatā*s. I will do whatever is required of me." Therefore, we need to go by the roles we are called upon to play. Every role one plays in real life has its own script. This script is to be construed as duty.

Our vision does not end with our own community, but covers the entire humanity, all the living beings. By doing what is needed, we will gain the greatest freedom. We become *brāhmaṇa* by disposition and as a *brāhmaṇa* we will discover the Lord, Brahman. When we have a mature mind, we enjoy the preparedness for the knowledge of oneself, the self that is non-separate from the very cause itself.

If everyone knows and performs his or her duties while playing a given role, then the question of right does not arise. One's duty towards the related other becomes the others' rights. The parents' duties towards their children would be the rights of the children and the duties on the part of the adult-children towards their parents become the parental rights. The same thing is applicable to all roles.

Here, we face certain questions. If the parents' expectations from their children are too many, to what extent the children are expected to comply with these expectations? They seem to be more than their normally expected duties. For instance, many parents consider that it is the duty of the children to get married. But they do not want to. Would it be right on the part of the parents to insist? We have to look into this and similar things in the light of what the *Bhagavad Gītā* has to say.

I think you need to understand this line from the *Bhagavad Gītā* (18.46): "*Svakarmaṇā tam abhyarcya siddhiṁ vindati mānavaḥ*, "Worshipping Him (the Lord) by one's duty one gains success (clarity of mind and thereby *mokṣa*)." Elsewhere also the *Gītā* says (3.35): "*Svadharme nidhanaṁ śreyaḥ paradharmo bhayāvahaḥ*, it is better for one to follow one's own duty, rather than following the duties of another which are fraught with pain."

What it really means is that you should not go by your likes and dislikes; instead, you have to go by what is right and wrong, in any given situation. The *Gītā* even goes to the extreme to say that it is better to die following your *dharma* than following your likes and dislikes if they are against *dharma*. Obviously, the *Gītā* wants that you cannot allow your likes and dislikes to dictate your life. You have to go only by what is right and wrong. Sometimes, likes and dislikes concur with rights and wrongs. Then there is no problem; what you dislike is wrong and what you like is right. Your action becomes spontaneous. On the other hand what is right is one thing and what you feel like doing is quite another, then what should you do? You should go by what is right. This is what is called deliberate action. Either your action should be spontaneous or it should be deliberate. You cannot try to be spontaneous. You are either spontaneous or deliberate.

As I am walking, if somebody falls down right in front of me, I will not wait for an introduction; I will reach out to help spontaneously. Let us take another scenario. A gentleman is well dressed and is on his way to an important dinner on a rainy day. On the way he sees someone falling on the slippery slushy road. If he helps him, sure his clothes will be ruined.

He will miss the important dinner where he would be meeting some important clients. That dinner could make a difference in his life. What should he do now? He looks around to see if there is anybody else to help him. Unfortunately, there is no one. Should he leave the poor man to his fate and carry on? He could rationalise his action by telling himself, 'If he is lucky, if fate so wills, someone will help him.' No, he cannot do that because he would not like someone do this to him. So, he has to act deliberately. In such a situation one does not go by one's likes and dislikes. One goes by what is right; what is right becomes one's duty. Sometimes, the duties concur with one's likes and dislikes, but more often than not, they do not. So, one has to deliberately choose an action. That is called duty. It is one aspect of *karma-yoga*.

In our culture, emphasis is more on duties than on rights. One's duty as a citizen towards the State and the State's duty towards the citizen will grant each other the rights naturally. Thus, the State's right is our duty and our right is the State's duty. Similarly, a neighbour, friend, employer, employee, father, and so on, all have duties, mutual duties.

The concept of duty works only when both the parties follow this principle of duty. Sometimes the problem comes when, for instance, a husband commands his wife, "This is your duty" forgetting he has his duties. The concept of duty works only when both the parties respect each other; otherwise we have to go by rights and enforce responsibilities. The State becomes the enforcer, and the individual loses the mature living of self-governance.

In a society where right is important, right is bound to be demanded, and the responsibility is likely to be forgotten. If duties are spelt out and we go by them, there is a possibility of meeting somewhere and the possibility of conflict is less, because duty means that which I have to do. We become humble too because we cannot fulfil all our duties. When you cannot fulfil your duties, you are humble, but if you demand rights, there is no humility. Where there is demand, there is aggression. The individual is aggressive; society is aggressive.

The Indian society is non-aggressive because of this emphasis on duty. You perform your duty and so does everyone else. In all the countries that became independent after the Second World War, there were coups except in India. The reason is obvious—the country is duty-bound.

Duty of husband and wife

Previously there was *varṇāśrama-dharma,* with duties well spelt out and each one knew what was to be done. Nowadays, we do not have that system working strictly. So, in a husband-wife relationship, should a wife remain at home, in a small flat, spend the whole day waiting for her husband to return? When he returns, suppose he is tired, is not disposed for any interaction with his wife, is she expected to be at peace with herself? How can she spend her time in a small flat where there is not even much household work to be done? Neither has she learnt any classical music nor any other fine art to spend time with. Now what should she do? What is her duty?

The best option I would say is to go out and work. This is how it should be. If she has children, it is a different thing. She will have enough to do, to be occupied meaningfully.

It is not an absolute pronouncement that a woman should remain at home, and that she should never leave the house. In an agricultural society, it was but natural for women to remain at home to take care of a number of things. Now here in a city, it is entirely a different situation. Therefore, if necessary, the wife should also work.

Duties are relative, time-bound. They are subject to interpretation, which changes from time to time. However, there is a spirit in the sense of duty, which never changes. The husband's duty towards his wife is to make her happy. That is the basic duty. Understand that as duty.

What is the husband's duty towards his wife? Is it to make her sad or to make her happy? Again, why should that woman get married to you? Is it to reap sorrow? She thought she would be happy with the man she married and that man thought he would be happy with her. Therefore, what can be the basic duty towards each other, other than making the other happy? It is better that you learn how to make the other happy. At least know how to avoid making the other person sad. If you know that, it is easy to make him or her happy. If each one attempts to make the other happy you will find that you meet the other somewhere. The criterion is not how much happiness you can get out of the other person, but rather how much happiness you can give to the other. That is what we call duty for a husband or wife, to make the other happy. In making the other happy any sacrifice is worthwhile. In fact, what is involved is not sacrifice at all; you enjoy the situation because the other is happy.

Only if the other is happy can you be happy because you are wedded to the other. Suppose, your wife is unhappy and she sits in one corner, can you be happy? If you are wedded to her, her happiness is your happiness. Is it not true? So, you cannot gain anything by making the other unhappy. It is better to make the other one happy and that involves no sacrifice at all, because there is self-interest. In your own self-interest you better make the other person happy. '*Ātmanastu kāmāya sarvaṁ priyaṁ bhavati*, it is only for the sake of the self does anything become an object of love.' Only for the husband's sake does the wife become the object of love. Similarly, for her sake he becomes the object of love. Everyone wants to be free and happy and comfortable. If I make the other person happy, I am only doing my duty. When we contribute towards and care for the happiness of the other person, most of our problems are solved.

The husband should know that his wife could never be happy without including in her life her parents and her siblings, just as he wants her to include in her life his parents and other members of the family. In patriarchy, the woman needs to include her in-laws, while her husband expects her not have anything to do with her family. He needs to include her family—that inclusion will make the marriage happy.

DUTY OF MOTHER-IN-LAW AND DAUGHTER-IN-LAW

In Indian household, the duty of a mother-in-law towards her daughter-in-law does not seem to be clear. A mother-in-law's duty is to provide support to the daughter-in-law to make her feel at home in the new environment. The problem with a mother-in-law is her possessiveness over her son. She thinks that her son is a part of her. No person is part of anyone. Each one is a complete person. One has to make one's life. Parents do not recognise this fact and, therefore, they suffer and make their children also suffer. They should gracefully retire. Then they will be sought for advice, for emotional support. Only then will there be harmony at home.

Every mother-in-law was once a daughter-in-law. It amazes me that she did not learn anything. It looks as though she is taking out the frustrations she suffered, on others. Parents create problems for their children, perhaps out of insecurity too. They make their son feel guilty. 'We brought you up, gave you education, gave this, gave that, yet you listen to your wife and do not care for us.' They manipulate the children through this type of emotional blackmailing. Is this proper? I would say that the parents' duty is to leave the children alone. Let them make or mar their lives. Did you give them education? Yes, you did. Did you at least try your best to bring them up properly? Yes, you did that too. Then, you have nothing more to do. Your duty is over.

Duty of parents towards children

Now the question is: Is it the parents' duty to see that their children are married? I say, definitely not. To educate the children is the only duty. Marriage is not your duty. Who are you to decide whether they should get married or not? Please understand that it is not your duty. In the Mogul period, young widows and unmarried girls faced the problem of forced marriages with Mogul soldiers. To avoid such a situation, the Hindu parents gave away their daughters in marriage when they were still children, playing with dolls. That is why giving away the daughter in marriage was called *kanyā-dāna*. *Dāna*, gift, is possible only when the *kanyā*, the girl, does not have her own choice. If the *kanyā* has her choice, then it is not a gift. Whatever you give should not disagree; he, she or it should not say, 'I will not go.' You cannot give away a thinking person as a gift. After the ban of child-marriage such marriages have almost disappeared. Girls are, generally, married after the age of 22. There is no *kanyā-dāna*, there is only *pāṇi-grahaṇa*. Both the bride and the groom are adults. Naturally, then the parents' attitude also must change.

Two types of marriage existed even in our ancient society. In one, the couple choose each other. In the other, the parents choose for them, though they are adults. In this type of arranged marriage there is an advantage. The parents are objective. They do not fall in love with the boy or the girl. They can enquire into the background and other details and ascertain whether the boy or girl is capable of leading a normal healthy life, whether there is any hereditary problem, and so on. Once the parents are satisfied, they settle the marriage.

Now, let us suppose the girl chooses the boy. What is the basis for her choice? She cannot choose him because he wears a butterfly shirt, tight pants and pointed shoes. All these perhaps reveal the type of person she wants to relate to, plus looks. More often than not she falls in love with a person like this. She does not know his parents, his background in terms of values, skills, commitments, culture, beliefs and so on, about him. She gets married but soon discovers that this person is incapable of earning and taking responsibilities. Married life becomes a tragedy.

When you choose a person, you get emotionally involved and lose your objectivity. When the parents choose, they are objective, being not emotionally involved. Therefore, they can be more practical. This is the difference.

In an arranged marriage, you accept a person as your partner in life, even before meeting him or her. It is only later, after the marriage, that you 'discover' the person chosen for you. Therefore, the marriage is likely to last happily. An American once asked me the reason for the seeming success of Hindu marriages. I answered that a Hindu loves the person whom he or she is married to whereas in the West one marries a person whom one thinks one loves. In such a marriage, the love born of superficial knowledge of the other is bound to be found wanting in depth and stability in the wake of more knowledge of the spouse. They try to get along for sometime. All that is there is sympathy, but sympathy is not enough to make a happy marriage. Soon the marriage ends in separation.

In arranged marriage, it is just the opposite. You accept the person first and discover the person later. The discovered person is loved in spite of his or her limitations, since the person has been already accepted.

Any type of marriage can last happily only when the couple accepts each other totally.

Love does not have any particular prerequisite other than a simple attitude of acceptance. If you have that attitude of acceptance, that love is simple—it can be towards a tree, a bush or a pet. You can discover love for any person; love is non-judgemental.

Therefore, you accept the person as the person is and there you find love. You love the person you marry. It works. Yes, in an arranged marriage there is this advantage, but it does not in any way mean that the parents can give away their children in marriage without respecting their inclinations. The parents have to tell the teenagers repeatedly what do they expect of them, in clear terms. They need to tell that seeking alliance in the same community is to find kinship. Let them also tell the children clearly what they do not want. The problem arises when they do not communicate to the children what do they want in the right age. One fine morning they say, "Now, you should get married to this girl" and the son says, "No, I am not interested in marriage." In fact, the boy wants to get married, but to someone else. He is afraid to say that to the parents and they too do not ask. When pressed, the boy says, "I want to marry this particular girl." The whole heaven comes down; there is shock, disappointment, hurt, tears and so on.

Children also have to respect the parents' background and act with responsibility. They cannot be happy hurting them.

Finally I say that it is nice to work for children's marriage but it is not to be looked upon as duty.

Duty of children towards parents

The next question is: What is the son's or the daughter's duty towards parents? Your duty as a son is to take care of the old parents. If you are married, living in a small flat and find that everyone cannot be huddled together in one place, keep the parents separate. Take care of them; that is what is important. If economically it is not possible to keep them separate, then have them with you. It is your duty as a son. If there are more children, let them all share the duty. Often what happens is that some of them make sure that the parents do not come to them. The parents are then stuck with one son. Slowly it becomes a problem for both the parents and the married son. In case it is inevitable that the parents stay with their son for economic reasons, then, as I said earlier, the parents should learn to live a quiet, retired life, a life of non-interference with regard to the children and their wishes. In fact, it is good to have such parents at home. Their guidance, their experience, their help, their affection for the children—all these will be a great blessing. But the parents should know how to conduct themselves. They should know how to remain away from becoming a problem to their children.

Duty of the citizen and the state

Let us see next, the citizen's duty towards the State. Every 5th year one has to cast one's vote to elect the Government in the Centre as well as in the State. Is this all? No, as a citizen, you have to raise your voice either to protest or to suggest. You can use the available media for the purpose. Burning buses or looting shops is definitely not the duty of a citizen. One has to participate in political affairs. At least one has to understand what is going on around.

However, do not mix religion and politics. Religion destroys politics and politics destroys religion. Keep religion where it belongs and it is beautiful. A religious person can be involved in political life, but let him or her not make religion an issue of politics. It becomes a big problem, and destroys religion in the process. Be a religious person, follow whichever religion you believe in and follow it well. Then, when there are political responsibilities, it is, in fact, a religious duty to fulfil them.

There is a great deal of inter-relationship among these various duties and you cannot categorically state a rule that will apply to everyone under all conditions. Be alert to the situation and find out exactly what you are required to do.

When you live in the society, you have to participate in the government in whichever manner you are called upon to. You cannot remain indifferent saying, 'It does not matter whether Rāma rules or Rāvaṇa rules, I still have to stand in the queue for the bus.' That is wrong thinking. At least, include in your daily prayers the country, the people and all living beings in general.

Svasti prajābhyaḥ paripālayantām
nyāyyena mārgeṇa mahīṁ mahīṣāḥ
gobrāhmaṇebhyaḥ śubhamastu nityaṁ
lokāḥ samastāḥ sukhino bhavantu

Let there be happiness for the people
Let the kings rule the earth with justice
Let there always be happiness for the *brāhmaṇas* (thinking people) and the cows
Let all the people be happy.

kāle varṣatu parjanyaḥ

pṛthivī sasyaśālinī

deśoyaṁ kṣobharahitaḥ

brāmaṇaḥ santu nirbhayāḥ

Let there be rain at proper time

May the earth bear good crop

May the country be free from disturbance

May the *brāhmaṇa*s (thinking people) be free from fear.

This is one kind of participation in politics. It is a political participation but in the form of prayer. Let there be happiness and welfare for all people. Let the rulers, the kings rule well the earth with justice. May the rulers always wield the sceptre of justice while ruling their respective countries all over the world. Let there be always happiness and care in the world for all the thinking people as well as the cattle. Let there be rain at proper time and in proper measure. Let there be no *ativṛṣṭi,* too much rain, or *anāvṛṣṭi*, no rain at all. Let the clouds bring rain in time. Let the earth bear good crop. Let the country be free from poverty, drought, and diseases. May all the thinking people be free from fear. Let there be freedom of speech. Let them express without fear and communicate what they think is right and what is wrong. This is the prayer, our daily prayer.

The State's duty is very clear. They have to provide the infrastructure for the people to live in peace and freedom. The problem with our State is that it wants to control everything. This style of governance infringes upon the freedom of people all the time. The State that infringes upon citizen's freedom is not a State. It should give its citizens the freedom; give them an infrastructure where they can grow. The citizen should be like a tree whose growth is not obstructed and which stands in its own glory.

When freedom is there, responsibility is often forgotten. Emphasise the responsibilities all the time. Make the people go by their responsibility. Do not let them get away with irresponsible actions. Educate them in terms of their responsibility, give them the freedom and you will find India a great country.

India does not have over-population. It only has extra population, which means we have extra hands and legs. Do not count only the mouths. Suppose, you have two extra hands on you. What will you do? Will you surgically remove them? If there are two more hands, you only have to organise them.

You should provide work for two more hands; otherwise they will get atrophied.

Understand that we have excess hands in the country. What we need is to get organised. Organise them well and we can beat all the countries in the world. No country can produce goods as cheaply as we can; we can beat them all, hands down. It is very simple, because we have so many hands and legs. We also have enough brains in this country. All that is required is organisation. I hope that we are going in that direction. Let us wait and see.

Role of values

The fact that you are born with a faculty of choice makes you a unique living being. As a human being, you can use, abuse, or disuse this faculty. In using this freedom of choice, you have no choice whatsoever. Every individual is given a set of norms on the basis of which he or she can exercise his or her choice. Knowledge of the universal matrix of values and value-based duties is inborn and understood with the help of common sense.

Further, common sense must be common to all. For instance, we know that we do not want to get hurt. Common sense allows us to appreciate that others also do not want to get hurt. No living organism wants to get hurt. Thus, not hurting, is one universal value. Similarly, as we do not want to be lied to, others do not want to be deceived by us. We do not want to be the object of anybody's hatred, anger, or jealousy; we want everyone to be sharing, loving and friendly. This means that we are absolutely certain about the ethical values we want to instil in people. We also know that others expect the same from us.

Even though you have this knowledge, you have conflicts regarding right and wrong and find yourself compromising the universal norms. The 'something' that makes you cut corners is the lack of assimilation of the knowledge of the universal matrix of values that can take place only by your own initiative. If right and wrong action is not assimilated properly, then you will always have conflicts.

The word, 'spontaneous' can be used as an attribute to an action only when that action is in conformity with what is right. What is to be done is duty. Maturity implies the assimilation of the knowledge that you cannot do otherwise. If you become incapable of going against duty, then you are mature, grown up. Human interaction becomes very simple for such an individual.

Assimilation of values

Conflict will remain as long as your assimilation of values is incomplete. It is natural to have a conflict in the beginning. If you act upon your desires and the actions are not consistent with the knowledge of right and wrong, *dharma-adharma*, there will be conflict before, during and after the actions. Moreover, every conflict, every compromise, will add up in one's psyche so that by the time one is thirty or forty, one is a personality. One has to assimilate the values.

As a human being, you have to fall back upon the knowledge of values and then see that your actions are in conformity with this.

Your life should be such that it helps you assimilate these values. Your own free will must initiate the thinking process. The Lord can only give you the common sense knowledge that is adequate to start your life, but to make your life free from conflicts, to grow further, you have to use your own reason and will. And there is no *dharma* other than God. God is more than *dharma*, but *dharma* is not other than God. When there is no discordance between the *dharma*, God, and you there is joy; there is beauty. You need not do anything else to enjoy, bringing beauty to your life.

The value of a value is to be understood in order not to cause conflict. A conflict in terms of value is due to overriding priorities of likes and dislikes. If they do not conform to *dharma* and *adharma*, you cannot avoid conflict. Therefore, until you assimilate the value of a value, you have to conform to *dharma*, exercising your will. In doing so, there is conflict initially, but not later. Once you have assimilated the value of a value, the value is you. Education lies not in preaching values, but in teaching the value of values.

The growth of a person or the degree of assimilation of a value is in terms of the enormity of loss one perceives when there is a compromise of a value. This is with reference to universal values, *sāmānya-dharma.* Since, in the vision of the Veda, human destiny is nothing but self-discovery, as a human being one has to grow. This inner growth has to be effected by our own initiative. To help us, the Vedas have evolved a system of duty, which is understood as *viśeṣa-dharma.*

Viśeṣa-dharma is based upon a social requirement. Every human being is born, not merely as an observer of the world, but with the faculties to be an active participant in the creation. Since we are living a symbiotic, interrelated life, our contribution may help us live, and may help others live. We are, thus, interconnected and the same person does not and cannot do all the jobs. Therefore, the Vedas outlines a beautiful system called *varṇa-dharma.* The translation of *varṇa* is not 'caste'. The word does not lend itself to English translation. If you are truly ready for this journey of inquiry, you will find this *varṇa* to be something beautiful to understand, as long as your vision is clear. *Varṇyate anena iti varṇaḥ*—that by which something is described is *varṇa.*

A colour is *varṇa* because it is helpful to refer an object. So too, certain duties and attributes are called *varṇa*s. An order based on these is *varṇa-dharma*. How can the word 'caste' convey all this?

In the vision of the Veda, self-growth is the aim that will lead you to self-discovery. Whether you say *dharma* or *karma* it is one and the same. *Dharma* in terms of its expression, in a given situation, becomes *karma*, what is to be done.

You are not born as a simple witness. If you were born only with sense organs and no hands or legs or stomach, and so on, you could be purely an observer and not participate in the world's activity. However, fortunately or unfortunately, you are born with a body-mind-sense complex and the power to create. You are endowed with a threefold power: the power to know and to remember, *jñāna-śakti*; the power to will and desire, *icchā-śakti*; and the power to act, *kriyā-śakti*. With these, every human being is a participant in the creation. If you look at the other living organisms in the world, you find that each one of them participates without transgressing its limit. It does exactly what is expected of it because it has no free will. A mango tree does not yield an apple. Similarly, every animal behaves exactly as it should. Each one participates and contributes what it must.

There is a peculiar problem when dealing with a human being, because one has free will. One also has to participate, which implies interaction. When you relate to the world, you are the invariable person while the objects you relate to are variable in nature. You perceive different objects that have varieties of forms and colours. All these are variables. Even your personal relationships with people are not always the same. To one person you are the son, to another person father, and yet another an employer and so on. Thus, every day you have many people to meet with and relate to. Yet, the person whom others relate to is always the same, and that is you. You are the father, the son. You are invariable. As you relate differently, it looks as though you also undergo a change relevant to the person to whom you are related.

Relating as a father or a son, you are invariable, but there is a variable factor with reference to the person you relate to. This 'I' becomes the father, 'I' becomes the son. 'I' am the same, but there are these relevant relative changes. Whether I live in the society or withdraw from it to become a renunciate, *sannyāsin*, I have to relate to the world. No one can avoid relating. In this relating, the invariable 'I' is different from the father or the son that I am. In the father the 'I' is present whereas in the 'I' the father is absent. In the son the 'I' is present, in the 'I' the son is absent. If the son is present in the 'I' then I will be an absolute son; that is, I am everyone's son, born of every creature there is. In the 'I', there is absence of father, son, employer, and so on. With reference to objects I become a liker and a disliker too. If, in the 'I' there is a liker, then I will like every creature in the world. But that is not so. Therefore, in the 'I' there is no liker, but in the liker there is the presence of 'I'. In the 'I' there is no disliker, but in the disliker there is the presence of 'I'. It is very clear that despite all these varieties of changes that I undergo, the invariable 'I' seems to be free from the attributes of those changes. This is the very essence of the Vedic vision and the *Bhagavad Gītā*.

Oṁ Tat Sat

Books by Swami Dayananda Saraswati

Public Talk Series :

1. Living Intelligently
2. Successful Living
3. Need for Cognitive Change
4. Discovering Love
5. Value of Values
6. Vedic View and Way of Life

Upaniṣad Series :

7. Muṇḍakopaniṣad
8. Kenopaniṣad

Text Translation Series :

9. Śrīmad Bhagavad Gītā

   (Text with roman transliteration and English translation)

10. Śrī Rudram

    (Text in Sanskrit with transliteration, word-to-word and verse meaning along with an elaborate commentary in English)

Stotra Series :

11. Dīpārādhanā
12. Prayer Guide

    (With explanations of several Mantras, Stotras, Kirtans and Religious Festivals)

Moments with Oneself Series :

13. Freedom from Helplessness
14. Living versus Getting On
15. Insights
16. Action and Reaction
17. Fundamental Problem
18. Problem is You, Solution is You
19. Purpose of Prayer
20. Vedanta 24x7
21. Freedom
22. Crisis Management
23. Surrender and Freedom
24. The Need for Personal Reorganisation
25. Freedom in Relationship
26. Stress-free Living
27. Om Namo Bhagavate Vāsudevāya
28. Yoga of Objectivity
29. **Bhagavad Gītā Home Study Course** (Hardbound 9 Volumes)

Meditation Series :

30. Morning Meditation Prayers
31. What is Meditation?

Essays :

32. Do all Religions have the same goal?
33. Conversion is Violence

34. Gurupūrṇimā
35. Dānam
36. Japa
37. Can We?
38. Moments with Krishna
39. Teaching Tradition of Advaita Vedanta
40. Compositions of Swami Dayananda Saraswati

Exploring Vedanta Series : (*vākyavicāra*)

41. śraddhā bhakti dhyāna yogād avaihi ātmānaṁ ced vijānīyāt

Books translated in other languages and in English based on Swami Dayananda Saraswati's Original Exposition

Tamil

42. Veeduthorum Gitopadesam (Hardbound 9 Volumes) (Bhagavad Gītā Home Study Course)

Kannada

43. Mane maneyalli adhyayana (Hardbound 5 Volumes) (Bhagavad Gītā Home Study Course)
44. Vedanta Pravesike

Hindi

45. Ghar Bhaite Gita Vivechan (Volume 1 available) (Bhagavad Gītā Home Study Course)
46. Antardṛṣṭi (Insights)

47. Vedanta 24X7
48. Kriya aur Pratikriya (Action and Reaction)

English

49. The Jungian Myth and Advaita Vedanta
50. The Vedantic Self and the Jungian Psyche
51. Salutations to Rudra
    (based on the exposition of Śrī Rudram by
    Swami Dayananda Saraswati)
52. Without a Second

Biography

53. Swami Dayananda Saraswati
    Contributions & Writings
    (Smt. Sheela Balaji)

Distributed in India & worldwide by
MOTILAL BANARSIDASS - NEW DELHI
Tel: 011- 23858335/23851985/23852747

Also available at :

ARSHA VIDYA RESEARCH
AND PUBLICATION TRUST
32/4 Sir Desika Road
Mylapore Chennai 600 004
Telefax : 044 - 2499 7131
Email : avrandpc@gmail.com
Website : www.avrpt.com

ARSHA VIDYA GURUKULAM
Anaikatti P.O.
Coimbatore 641 108
Ph : 0422 - 2657001
Fax : 0422 - 2657002
Email : office@arshavidya.in

ARSHA VIDYA GURUKULAM
P.O.Box 1059. Pennsylvania
PA 18353, USA.
Ph : 001-570-992-2339
Email : avp@epix.net

SWAMI DAYANANDA ASHRAM
Purani Jhadi, P.B. No. 30
Rishikesh, Uttaranchal 249 201
Telefax : 0135-2430769
Email : ashrambookstore@yahoo.com

AND IN ALL THE LEADING BOOK STORES, INDIA